the words i
wish i said

by caitlin kelly

for you.

!

warning:
this book addresses a lot of
controversial subjects, and touchy
topics.

so to the close-minded people:
there's your warning.

!

table of contents:

author's note

.... 5

chapter 1: saving myself.

.... 7

chapter 2: you will never know.

.... 55

chapter 3: the darker pages.

.... 170

chapter 4: realizations.

.... 215

chapter 5: questions of this small world.

.... 236

author's note.

when i wrote my first book, <u>the words of a madman</u>, i never felt like it was finished. i wanted to add more, i had so much more to add. and my friends just said, why not write another book? i feel like there's so much in my mind, and so much poetry i'm constantly writing that i don't think i'll ever feel finished with simply one book. i'm sixteen years old. my book, <u>the words of a madman</u> was written mainly when i was fifteen and sixteen. these are the words i try to hold back from saying. these are the words that could break things when they are the happy days. these are my thoughts tracked down almost every day. these are the words i wish i said. not just to one person, but in general. writing helps give me a voice, so these are the words i wish i could say, but i hold back. i'm living life on strings now. but the most beautiful words are the words you fear to say. the words you have trouble saying because you can feel them rather than voice

them. the words that can't quite fit under a specific word, because these words are felt rather than said. these, well, these are the <u>words i wish i said.</u>

enjoy.

-   *caitlin kelly*

chapter 1.
saving myself

this chapter is about saving yourself when
no one else will. they can't hear the demons
taunting you in your head and they can't feel
your heart weeping through the silence.
sometimes the princess in the tower doesn't
need a prince, sometimes the evil queen
doesn't trap her up there. sometimes she
traps herself in the small, tall tower
overlooking the gray skies. and sometimes
they won't hear her cry for help. this is the
time where the little princess decides to save
herself. sometimes she isn't even a princess,
she's just a girl with a wandering mind. she
can fight the demons herself and she can
climb down herself. it takes time. but she
can do it. this chapter is about saving
yourself so no one else has to.

the ghosts are back

\-   my mental health

i'm just taking my time
learning how to fly.

confidence is a
nightmare
to insecure men.

he tried to fight for you
but he didn't fight hard
enough
he didn't seem to sharpen
his sword, instead
he lost the
battle
and you were left in the
castle

you don't need
someone to save
you from the tower

just *save yourself.*

02.09.2018

use your words caitlin

*jealousy
is a garment
most worn
under the
layers of
our soul
because no
one will
ever admit
when
they're
jealous.*

i'm
addicted
to
the feeling
of
adventure.

<u>who am i to you?</u>

i'm scared to love,
it's bad,
i'm protecting myself
so i'm
so
very
sorry
for
you,
trying to
love someone
broken
like
me.

it's
not
you

it's me.

my imaginary
friend
would be happy
to hear
my adventures
but it's too bad
he's left
a long time ago

-   adulthood

in
time
you
will
be
fine

is it me?

it can only get better from here

-    positive thoughts

i'm really
really
good at
lying

i've been
telling people
"i'm fine"
now for
four years

it must suck that life
is so painful to the ones
that try to
enjoy it

- dn#1

it's like i'm sitting in
a crowd of people
on the bleachers,
but i still feel
like there's no one
there

-    empty

they keep
saying it
will get better
but
when?

being alone
and
feeling lonely
are
two different
things

she is blooming
from the walls that
she sits against
no one else can
feel her presence
but i can see it

-    *the wallflower*

something
that's sad
is when you
know
someone's
falling in love
with you
but you're
sitting there
afraid of falling
for them
because
you're
not prepared
to be
hurt again.

~~maybe i'm the madman~~

the loudest silence is
when everyone's left you
and you don't know
why

-    thoughts that haunt me

god
dammit
why is my mind so full of thoughts
irrelevant to this,
my imagination is going
wild
and i'm trying to pay
attention to
my math homework.

stop
trying to
please
everyone,
caitlin

sticks and stones
may break my bones
but
words will
always
hurt me

la tristesse durera toujours

it's moments like this
when you're in complete
solitude
when you realize
how lonely you
really are

-    *alone and lonely are two different things.*

it's like i'm alone
but i don't want anyone
i'll push everyone away
i can't deal with anyone
i can't do it
i don't wanna be here
maybe
someone will
just sit with me
in complete silence
and maybe i'll be okay

let me
take care
of myself

before i
promise
to take
care of you.

bravery
is
when
you
ignore the
demons
taunting
you in
your head
and
you
move on
with your
day.

i'd love to see
how you see me
through
your eyes.

**i feel
numb,
i can't feel
my emotions
my body
my heart,
i act like it's there
like i'm fine
but honestly
my own brain
is confusing
me.**

they all ask me
where do you see yourself in ten years?

i honestly
don't know
because
a year ago
i wouldn't
see
myself here.

reflect now.

i can't stand
the judgmental
looks
they give me
or
the pity
in their
eyes
just
please
stop
worrying about me

she jumped off the plank
and dived in with the sharks
little did they know
a small weak girl like her
had a heart
and the sharks in the
water were nothing compared
to the ones swimming the
the depths of her
thoughts

- *she lived*

i'll keep writing you
poetry
even when my hands
can barely move
and you can't make
out the handwriting

if i "needed you"
like you keep stating
to everyone
then how come
i was alive way before
you came into my life
and i was able
to smile before i
was told i was
beautiful

-    i was my soulmate before anyone else was

i was an ocean
full of depth and beauty
but you
were afraid
of the sharks

how did i stay alive
if i didn't even
write?

she's so delicate
but her love
burns so hard

she gets broken
only trying to
give all her love

you give too much of yourself
to them and they'll
end up wanting more,
until you lose
who you
are.

humming to
love songs
by
myself

i'm flying above
watching all on the ground
weep

and i think,
why be sad?
there's a whole world
out there

then i wake up
and
i'm the one weeping
on the ground

where the fuck
are you peter pan?

you said you'd come
back for me.

-   first boy to lie

i know what i need
so stop telling
me otherwise.

spoiler alert:
she still lived.

chapter 2.

you would never know.

this chapter is the one that is the most
painful to organize. this chapter is for the
love poems. the ones you wish you could
erase, but they were true. and they were
written on these sad pages. sometimes you
wish you could erase their face from your
memories, because sometimes you think
you'd be better off without their face
replaying in your thoughts at night. but you
don't regret them, because when you look
back on the memories you're reminded that
there's someone that amazing out there. and
maybe this time it didn't work, but maybe
one day you'll find someone better for you.
this is the chapter for the love poems you
dread to look back on and refresh yourself
on how much you miss them. and yes. you
do miss them. and you're allowed to say
that, even if they don't miss you.

i can't
believe
your
cold
hands
can bring
so
much
warmth
to
my
heart.

i'm shivering
walking to
my car
and you
force me
to take
your jacket
and you
put it upon me

thank you,
for actually
caring
and pushing
through
my
stubbornness

i can't
believe
i
met
someone
like you
even
after
what i've
been through.

family can mean
anyone
you're
willing to
fight for.

you're my family now.

because
we'd all do
anything for you

anything you need

we're always here for you.

you
had a house
built out of bricks
and cement that only
ended up being abandoned

he
built me a house
with his own hands
out of sticks and mud
that is full of more
life
than any other
house on the road.

- *money isn't everything.*

with a tear
he whispers goodbye
and she sits there
watching the spark
leave his eye

i'm
not sure
what
love is
cause my
mind has fooled
me before,
 but
if this
is what i think
it is
then,
i'm in love
with you

i fell in
love with your
mind and
soul before
i fell in
love with
what's
in your
wallet
and your
pants.

true.

your heart is
almost
as empty
as your
promises.

__i wish i could__
__freeze time__
__and be in this__
__moment__
__with you__
__all my life.__

society's perspective
on beauty
isn't even based
on a person's
soul anymore
it's based on
their large
ass
and
tits.

he loves me...
    (passion in eyes)
he loves me not...
    (emptiness in words)
he loves me...
    (drunken touch)
he loves me not...
    (scattered texts)
he loves me...
    (lips pressed)
he loves me not...

\-   **the petals**

the nighttime
is so silent
i feel
so calm
just
writing
poems
about you
while
you're
asleep

what ever happened
to you and me?

betrayal.
verb

expose to danger by treacherously giving
information to an enemy

i hope you learned a lot of lessons from me
but i bet you didn't learn a thing.

the words i wish i said   caitlin kelly

love letters
on the floor
oh i really wish
you were knocking
at my door

roses are red
violets are blue
and i think i'm
in love with you.

the words i wish i said   caitlin kelly

even if you broke my heart into
tiny
little
pieces,
i'd still never
talk shit
about you.

   -    *there's none to say*

i'm confused
you're nice to me
to my face
you're all sweet
and lovely
but
as soon as
i turn around
it's like
you're
someone
different
talking to
others
about me.

- *two faced*

even after all that
i can still
look into your
eyes and be
unable to
hold back
a smile.

i've tried everything i love
even harder
over and over
just hoping that one day
you will get off the
top of my list

but after all this,
i'm not sure
you'll want
me anymore.

my feelings haven't faded
in fact they've grown
it's sad to know you've
gone in a different direction

je te veux toujours

i'm not here
cause i like you
i'm just
kissing you
because you're
lips are convenient
as his
are
not
here

- *a rebound*

it hurts

-   when you're taken for granted

we both thought we were on the same page
but it turns out
we're reading different stories

it's you
it's always been you
it will always be you

my imagination
must be
wild
if i still
think
you're
coming
back

it's really all about
who's the last one
on your mind before
you go to sleep.

-   it's always you

i can distract myself by watching movies
i can distract myself by making films
i can distract myself by listening to music
or talking to new people
or playing with my cats
but what it really comes down to
is what's on my mind when
i'm sitting all alone in my
car and usually
it's you.

we can't skip the
hard part
because it's gonna
help us
grow

you deserve more
than the kind
words i write about
you on paper
you deserve the whole
world wrapped in tissue
and a bow
for just breathing
this air
and being a glorious
sight to see on this
earth.

love.

the little cafe before we went to lay on the beach

the tidepools where we adventured

the place i call "lookout point"
with my favorite view

are all great places we've been

but my favorite place
is anywhere with you.

i stare into space
when i'm with you

you ask me
what i'm thinking

i'll smile and say nothing.

let me let you in on a little secret.
i'm thinking of you
i'm in love with you
and
my anxiety is making it hard for me to admit
i'm sorry
you probably think something is wrong. but my
mouth isn't allowing those three words
out of my mouth

oh boy.
it's true
i really do
love you.

every time
you say
you love
me
it feels
like the
first time
those
words
came
out of
your mouth.

- it's never too much

1.) what's a break supposed to do?
2.) how long?
3.) do you even want me?
4.) is this a break or break up?
5.) do you think i'm the best for you?
6.) why?
7.) okay, i understand. sorry for bothering you

-   how i picture the conversation

i've almost finished putting
the puzzle
together
the only
missing piece
is you.

02.11.2018

i'm ready whenever you're ready. i've set
everything up perfectly for when you come back.
but for some reason, there's a voice in the back of
my head, telling me you'll never come back, and
you'll move on, i mean, after all, that's what they all
did. but hey, if it's different, i'm ready for you.
i'm always ready for you.

timeless
eternity.

i'm writing so much about you, and i don't **ever**
want you to see it. because i know it's not your fault
and i know my words are harsh, it's mostly the
scenarios that are being made up in my head
about you
and i sure hope they don't end up becoming true.

what
      did
            i
                  do?

-    let me know so i can fix it

as soon as you
show someone
that you'd
do anything
for them
then they
may take
that to
their
advantage.

loving used to
be so easy
why is it
so difficult
now?

but why do we need a break
if it was all okay before?
we'll just end up
exactly where we were.

why do you still walk near me
but act like i'm nothing
you are so dull now
i want to say something
but my lips can't make a sound.

you turned right
into the words
you said
you'd never
be.

i still want to be with you
even though your feelings aren't true.

~~i like~~   ~~i really care~~
~~i strongly appreciate~~   ~~i miss~~
                                      ~~i really like~~
~~i admire~~   ~~i want~~

i love you.

maybe i did something
maybe you just realized
maybe i hurt you
maybe i'm the bad guy
maybe you're better off without me

- maybes

stranger -> close -> stranger

i keep quietly thinking to myself
i can't wait to tell you about this
but then i realize
you left
and i lost my
bestfriend.

love
is
more
than
just
a
four
letter
word.

you fall in love like how
you catch your breath,
slowly then all at once,
and you don't realize
you're in love until it
leaves you once again.

space is when the relationship isn't working
space is when you're tired of fighting
space is when you both need time
space is when you can't heal together
space isn't what i need
space is what you say you need
i guess we weren't on the same page.

the only thing
coming out of your
mouth
is complete
and utter
bullshit.

oh honey.
you keep
falling for
the boys
that believe
love is just
a
word.

i wish i could stop writing about you
but my words seem to sing
their own tune

you get over them like this- at first, you can't. his name is repeated over and over inside your little brain, singing a tune to you. until your heart gets bored of the tune that only ends up breaking you. one day at a time, you get over them when you stop searching for them in a crowd. you get over them when every love song on the radio is just another song. you get over them when every place you went is just a new place to make memories in. one day at a time. you get over them slowly, you get over them by focusing on your friendships, you get over them by focusing on your family. you get over them by loving yourself. you get over them by yourself, not latching onto a new one. you get over them when you realize your worth is not another person. you think you're over them, until you catch sight of them in a crowded starbucks or sometime in your day, and you can't explain why it hurt you, you thought you were over them. until, you see them and all the memories you had flushed your head and you remember how much you miss them. one day at a time. you get over them by doing everything else you love hoping that their name will disappear from the top of that list. you get over them when you realize they left you for a reason, and maybe that reason means they won't come back. ever. you get over them when you realize you both were reading different books but thought your page was the same.

*fill in
the
missing
halves*

it's like you've
killed
all the butterflies
in my
stomach
but i still
love you.

   -   *abuse*

just loving
like i
haven't been
hurt

you can't force or convince anyone to love you.
they'll figure it out themselves.

relationships are
like building a house together
there are little fights
big fights
agreements
happiness
and when the house is finished
that's like marriage,
after it's done
you both will make
minor renovations
or large ones
and you'll live in that
house
hopefully
for the rest of your lives

i love you

\-   *wow.*

i'm not mad
i'm just hurt.

when you smile
my heart just
fills up
with joy

my mind is so
consumed of
thoughts of
you and me
and what we
could've been
if you
didn't leave.

"they *always*
come back."

-   just not this time

i see why they call it
falling in love
because it's hard
to catch yourself
past a certain
point and
once you fall
it takes a fucking
long time to
pick yourself
back up
but when you're
in love
you feel as if
you're flying
soaring
out of the
cliff
you fell
down.

you may have broke my heart,
but of course i'm so messed up,
i still want to show you i care.

\- i'll never fucking learn

i wanna cry with you
but i can't
because if i was
with you
i wouldn't
be able to
hold back
a smile.

i just have to be the
stronger person
and hold my own
ground against
all these
threats you're
throwing at
me

you just make my
lips form into
this natural form
and i don't
know how

-   smile

you

-   *the greatest single word poem*

above all,
you're the one
i never
want to
lose.

-    but i still did

you said you lost
who you were with
me.

is that my fault?

i want you to want me

it's always easier said
than done,
it's easier to say you love
someone
yet turn your back on them in their
time of need
but it's harder to love them
and leave
the remains of their name
out of that
wonderful brain

i support you
and any decision
you make
even if that means
hurting me.
i still love you.

i never thought it
would've ended this
way
or this
fast.

you and i
were never
meant to
be

even if
we wanted
to
be

please
please
don't
leave
me

they say that if it's meant to
be then they'll come back,
contrary
i believe if they really loved
you then they would never
have left.

love is when
you run out of
things to do,
yet you never
grow bored of
one another

-   *you grew bored*

leave me if
that's what
you really
want.

\-   it could still work.

every tear out of
my eye
has your
name on
it.

i'll pretend i don't care
because
it seems to you like
i'm not there

please tell me
it will
all be okay

to the boy i still love -

i'm sorry

02.08.2018

we all mess up,
we're humans

sometimes i feel like i mess up beyond the
boundaries of stupidity

all i know is that i follow my gut instinct
and it doesn't lead me in the
best direction always...

sometimes i hope you put mayonnaise on your fries and your mind wanders to the thought of me. sometimes i hope you see a clear blue sky and you remember my eyes lighting up for such a nice day. sometimes i wonder if you still remember my face in all the memories we had. sometimes i wish you were still here, but if you wanted to be then you would be. you chose to leave, oh well.

not talking to me
leads you
nowhere

true love
is fighting
through
the hardest
of situations

-    *guess it wasn't true to you.*

the words i wish i said   caitlin kelly

should of
stuck with my
gut instinct

you always ask me
what does the "look" mean?

"the look" means
i can't believe someone
as amazing as you
is spending their time with
someone like me

"the look" means
i look at you and can see you
as the only person in the world

"the look" is
when i can't describe
in words
how much

i love you.

the words i wish i said   caitlin kelly

how'd i end up
so lonely again?

don't give up on me
i could be what
you need

you're a
walking
masterpiece

so many constant thoughts
in my mind

constantly hurting me

repeating the words you told it

we're sitting
in a field
of dandelions
and grass

just watching
the time
tick away and
pass

i keep on having this recurring dream, that i see
you in the distance and naturally i start walking to
you. and as i get closer and closer i make eye
contact with you and i fall down, this deep hole...
then i wake up. the last image in my head in the
morning is you watching me fall so helplessly down
this hole, screaming and shouting. and you watch
my with no expression, and no sense to help me.
- maybe it foreshadowed something?

the words i wish i said   caitlin kelly

if it was
easy to
move on
then it
wouldn't
be love
would it?

i wrote you two love poems yesterday
i wrapped them together,
          put a bow around them and i was going to
hide them somewhere you'd find.

the hope from yesterday made me so inspired, i
thought i'd do something for you

this morning was my first heartbreak you've given
me,
i say first because even in the slight chance you
come back, i know i won't refuse

i need you
          even as a friend

i don't need time to myself
          please see that

you can come back and hurt me all you want
and what i know is
i'll never stop loving you

          -    a tragedy

this heartbreak is
nothing like the others

because this heartbreak
is something that
i know you
wouldn't have
chosen.

-    sucks

i just wanted to let you know,
i'm *always* here for you,
whenever you need me

please just dm me, and
i'll answer,
even if you just want to talk about your day or
something silly

i'm here for you
and
i'm not leaving anytime soon
(unless you want me to)

-    i'll never stop loving you

"i'll never hurt you"

"i'll never leave you"

- top two biggest lies even if it's not
intentional

i hate it.
i hate still being in love with you
i know it's not your fault
and i really do wish i was still in your arms

but hey
maybe one day it will work

maybe time is what we need

-    optimism

i'd still fight
for you
but i
don't know
if you want
me
to

i'd still do anything
for you
but i
don't know
if you want
me
to

black and white
but that's not
life

-    the grey area

do you ever
love someone
so much that
you only want the
best for them?

then you come to the
realization
that maybe you
aren't the best
for them.

-    most heartbreaking conclusion

they say if you love something,
then set it free
but
why has that
made us both
unhappy?

now you're just a
stranger
with all my
secrets
and
dreams

if something breaks your heart,
then why do you keep watching?

"because we're hoping for
a different outcome."

i thought i was okay

until i saw your face

i'm not the girl that a boy will chase from side of the
world to the other. i'm not the girl that all the boys
praise and describe her with words like "perfect".
i'm not the girl boys would wait a lifetime for. i'm not
the girl you'd see in a romance movie that doesn't
have a sharp bone existing in their body. i'm not the
girl they'll follow all the way to the airport to say
goodbye to. i'm not the girl they'll stand outside the
window with a radio for. i'm not the girl they'll ever
need. i'm just the girl they'll waste their days with
until the right one comes around. i'm just the girl
they'll leave when things get hard. i'm just the girl to
pass their time.

they say they'll never leave you
until they do
even if they don't want to
they think they know what's best for you

-    they don't

for the boy i still love,

i've written more poetry about you
and you wouldn't have a clue
the fact that i still love you
more than you ever knew.

my heart isn't messed up by your thought
but by the memories in my mind
your face
your touch
your smile
oh god that smile.
the one i could stare at all night and all day

i've never gotten over you
because i've never felt the need to
just the thought of you
makes me sing a tune
just a picture makes me smile
even though it should make me die a little

just you.
the thought that we could still be what we once were
just the *hope* in my eyes
that one day i'll have you back.

but what kills me is that
i can't reserve you
because you're not a library book or
a table at a crowded restaurant

and worst of all,
you're not mine,
anymore.

"it wasn't us"
            i keep telling myself
"it wasn't me"
            i keep telling myself
"it was the timing"
            i keep telling myself

yet my messed up mind will tell me that
you could find someone to love you more

that no matter how many times you told me i was
perfect
i knew you could find someone else

i may love you more than words can describe
and that won't ever let me stop thinking about you at
night

i've written so much poetry about you
and you wouldn't have a clue.

i thought you'd
be my everything
but you only
left me with
nothing.

our hearts both
broke different ways,
sadly…

now our broken pieces don't
fit together like
a puzzle

-   we have to find our missing piece
elsewhere.

sorry if that was
too much

spoiler alert:
as much as she wanted him
she never *needed* him

chapter 3.

the darker pages.

beware:
this chapter is for the darker pages. the
pages people don't dare write about. these
are the pages that make me different.
because i'm not hiding them in the shadows
anymore. i've written these but i've never
shown them to a soul. this is the time i'm
showing them. the best advice i've gotten is
write about what you're most scared to say.
here's what i'm scared to say. i'm scared
about the people that will perceive me
different after reading these. that will show
their pity in their eyes. *i don't want your
pity.* these are the pages that no one talks
about. a trigger warning: these pages may
get too much at times, these pages are here
to show you that these are real feelings and
thoughts. if you are feelings suicidal please
find help, or call the hotline. and please
please understand that you are not alone.
you're never alone. even though out of the 7
billion on the planet you feel like you're
suffering in silence, you aren't. **enjoy the
darker pages.**

national suicide prevention hotline:
1-800-273-8255

entry: 02.07.18 one of the darker days

i don't think i've felt this alone for a while. i woke up
this morning, three hours before my alarm, hoping,
praying that nothing happened. that i would wake
up on tuesday, february sixth and realize it was all
just a nightmare. but it wasn't. that was reality. i'm a
stupid teenager. i may even be a slut, who knows?
but why does _my life_ have to follow a plan? why am
i treated like a puppet? why am i not good enough
in their eyes? my mind is common to overthinking..
my mind is prone to insanity. the cuts i lay upon my
thigh and arms aren't even a little pain that i'm
feeling in my head. most times i wonder why i
haven't killed myself yet. i was so happy but now
i'm so so very sad. i don't think my happiness ever
stays long, i don't think it will ever stay long. the
sadness always comes back to haunt our minds.
the pain will never go away
la tristesse durera toujours
{ the sadness lasts forever }

sometimes i wonder why people look at death like
it's a tragedy. it's not the tragedy, it's everything
leading up to it that is the tragedy.

188

~~maybe we're the bad guys~~

i don't know what hurts more
my heart
or
my brain?

- confusion

take a gun
to my head
because i'd be
better off
dead.

i wish i
could take
a knife
and end my
life.

okay i've had my fun
-     suicide

even the
happiest of
times are
just false
reality

***maybe if i just
kill myself then
you can stop
worrying about
me.***

hurts like hell.

-   missing you

;

to clarify why the last page was a single semicolon.
a semicolon is when an author could've chosen to
end their sentence, but they did not.

let it sink in

you know i was in love with you, right?

"and what changed?"

nothing.

maybe
~~insanity~~
is underrated.

the words i wish i said   caitlin kelly

i'm strong
you've never
seen me weep
even after all this
and that's because as
soon as you walk away i'll
be weeping harder than you'll
ever know, but i'm strong enough
to hold it in so it will never hurt you.

let me eat enough food
so i can drown in my sorrows

<u>taunt my corpse</u>

-   *they'll never learn*

i'll be okay

just maybe not today

grades are
more important
than my
mentality

2:45 pm
caitlin, stop opening up and trusting them, they end up breaking you more and more until one day you'll be nothing.

the words i wish i said   caitlin kelly

i'm not
perfect
and
i never
will be

unrequited love
is the one
that fucks us
all up.

my hearts thrown
in the gutter
again.

dragons are the boys that
promise you everything
but leave you with
nothing

i'm making promises to you and you won't even
see.

broken hearted
writing letters
to boys
that they'll
never see
oh god,
it's hell
being sixteen.

i would die for you
if you want me to

i would fight for you
if you want me to

i would lie for you
if you want me to

but would that all
be the same
for you?

the words i wish i said   caitlin kelly

it's been four years
and i still
don't want to
be here

~~all the words i wish i said.~~

silently screaming.

i just want him
he's the only thing on my mind
even if i try to think of anything else
my mind wanders back to the thought
of him.
i'm starting to think
i'm going insane
and to escape
the thoughts of him
are only if
i blow my fucking brains out.

the words i wish i said   caitlin kelly

twinkle twinkle little star
let me get hit by a car
jump off a roof and try to fly
oh god i wish i could die
twinkle twinkle little knife
help me end this wretched life.

don't you fucking mind?

i keep letting them hurt me
and i'm doing
nothing to stop
it.

the words i wish i said   caitlin kelly

you're
        killing
                              me
                                    with
                                          all

the
                        silence.

i carve lines
and act like
i'm fine.

how selfish
would i be
if i just
decided
to leave?

why me?

hey
hey
hey
guess what
i'm a human
being
too!!

they ask me
how i am
i say
i'm tired
but they
aren't
asking me
what i'm
tired
of.

sometimes i wonder who i am... well most times. i've become so accustomed to wearing masks around different people and faking a smile with so much pain... that, i ask myself: who? am? i? i have to take that step back, evaluate, and decide. what makes me... me? what qualities do i have? how do other perceive me? i end up getting to the conclusion to stop getting in my own head and being silly. to sit back and relax. but i'm one of the rare few that has so much trouble relaxing. my mind wanders.... i'm a dreamer they say. i think too in-depth. oh well.

undeveloped polaroids
unspoken words
untouched hearts
unmarked maps
unclear messages

- path to a broken soul

her smile shines
bright

because she doesn't
want anyone
to see the
pain under it

she's sick

sick of all the lies
sick of being let down
sick of putting her all into something
that just hurts her more

she's sick

i'm sick of
choosing which
mask i'll wear each
day
because i'm afraid
of showing
my true self
to the ones who
will try to take
advantage of
it.

spoiler alert:
she's still
alive.
and sometimes,
just sometimes…
she lets out a smile.

chapter 4.

realizations.

this chapter is about the realizations you
make after an incident. when you thought
everything was great until you look deeper
into it. yes. these are some words i wish i
didn't write. but that's what they are. you
don't ever want the harsh realizations, you
always want the sugarcoat. but once again,
these are the words i'm afraid to write. these
are the realizations that sometimes haunt me
at night. these are the poems that hurt to
look back on. in fact, these are the words i
wish i *didn't* say. since when i wrote them
they were my "mind overthinking" but they
became true. not every single one. just some.
but still. wow. didn't think i could predict
the future that well. enjoy this chapter of
realizations.

my mind is gonna
explode
with all the
thoughts of what
we could've
been.

10:55 pm

missing you usually comes in showers
tonight is a thunderstorm

the words i wish i said   caitlin kelly

talk
    to
        me

didn't know
i was so
disposable

he is the poem
i wouldn't dare
to write
i would push through,
scared,
to see the words
i chose
because he
was the one
i was madly in
love with even
if i wouldn't admit
it.

the words i wish i said   caitlin kelly

i can't be your hero

you think it's
all a game
and i'm
your
favorite
card to
play.

i hate to say it
but sometimes
i feel like i didn't exist in your
life because you loved me
i feel like i exist in your life
for the attention you crave
and the gap of loneliness to fade

i don't hate you
i just hate that
i can't have you

you only loved me
when i was weak
because it
made you feel
better
about
yourself.

i'll never hate you
even if i act like
i do.

he was the whirlwind
that swept me off
my feet
but only ended up
leaving me
to weep.

"how'd you know it was over"

when his eyes stopped lighting up.

i tried drinking
i tried driving 100 on the freeway
i tried extreme sports
but nothing will be the
same as when my heart was next to yours

the only thing that's your fault
is making me fall
so goddamn head over
heels for you.

the words i wish i said   caitlin kelly

their opinions are only attempting to burn through
the pages of our love story

*but babe, they haven't seen the pages that are far
from flammable.*

why were
you able
to move
on so
quickly if
i was the
one you
loved?

why am i always the one
left heartbroken?

you're probably
more in love
with the memories
than the person
you created them
with.

i can't believe this
but i'm used to
getting what's
unexpected.

spoiler alert:
sometimes realizations and overthinking
become your best friend. sometimes it helps
you predict what's going to happen before it
does. even though, you hope that they'll
never happen, they still do. sometimes as
much as you hate overthinking, you won't
be caught off guard.

chapter 5.

questions of this small world.

this chapter is about the questions of this small world. since the other chapters were about your own world in you head, i thought, why not make one about the actual world. either made up. or living. sometimes i don't like this world, and i don't understand it. so i make up my own. and it's easy because i can make up my own rules and my own thoughts. and all the negative people are out of it. my world inside my head is wild, but if i ramble on about it it will be the size of another book. (maybe i should write one). this chapter is about the messed up beautiful world we live in. and it's about the world up in our brains.

it's fucking terrible to love someone
but live in fear that they're
going to leave or hurt you.

we'll break someone else's heart
before they break ours.

because we're scared
we don't want to be the one hurt,
or broken

we'd rather be the asshole that dumped someone.

what a fucking cruel world.

i don't like the world
so i made up my own

the world relies so much on money,
and material items
i get essentials
but..
the five dollar dress i get from
goodwill is just as good
as the fifty dollar dress you buy
somewhere else.

it's just fabric

my car works just fine.
would i like a new one?
yeah probably.
do i need a new one?
no.

it's just an object.
it's just material.

adventures and experiences are *way better* than
those two thousand dollar gucci slippers you "need"

flying to see your family is way better than your
two hundred thousand dollar lamborghini

yeah, cool car, we get it, you have money

grow up, stop basing life on materials and
live a goddamn life.

after time,
sorry loses
it's value that
it once had
it loses it's
power to
recover the
ashes of
the heart

01/17/2018

i saw a tweet the other day that said

"break her heart and she's yours forever"

the point of this frustrated me so much. it clearly
shows how some people only truly date for
attention. it's disgusting how you can even **want** to
break someone's heart. they invest time into your
crusty ass and you're over here sending tweets
about breaking their heart.
you attention-seeking whore.

love is about building each other.
not breaking one for attention.

humankind
is now
so
absorbed in
their phones
like
hi?
i'm right here,
a human
to talk to
right in front of you

the reason why relationships don't last nowadays is
that when the "spark" is gone, they find it boring.
the start of relationships are almost always fun. but
real love is sticking there with the person through
all the ups and downs, through the good and bad.

real love is loving someone through their best and
through their worst.

real love is building each other up.
real love is staying there even when the "spark" is
gone.

i may not know much about "love" because i'm
some stupid adolescent

      but if i know anything about love

it's that you'll stay no matter what.

the words i wish i said   caitlin kelly

if you voice
your thoughts and emotions
and he fears it
then he has no
reason to hear it

what if
what is isn't
what is isn't
what's impossible is possible
what's possible is impossible
and what's imagination is reality
and what if mere reality is just our imagination

01.29.2018

coach put me in
i need to run
and we may not win
but isn't it all about the fun?

almost all children had an
imaginary friend
i didn't.
i had an imaginary "monster"
i eventually became
comfortable
with fearing it and
dealing with the pain it caused
and eventually, i became
comfortable of being attached to it

i guess that's why
i'm so attracted to
boys with empty hearts
that make empty promises

because i've
became so
accustomed to
dealing with
pain.

learn the most
from
the ones we
hate the most

what if
my green
is
your
blue

-   *sorry*

there's
a difference
between
living
and
existing

spoiler alert:

these were not all the words i wish i said. in
fact most of these words i wish i *didn't*
write. just to the small fact of, i wish i didn't
care… but sadly i do. but if i said the words
i wish i did, then they wouldn't be my little
secret, they would be words on paper in a
book. they would be words taken out of
context, because the world loves to take
things out of context. the words i wish i said
are between me and my party of a brain.
because if you knew the words, then you
would have such an advantage over me, and
my quiet showers where i ramble on to
myself about my words wouldn't be my
secret anymore. you may be able to take
most of me but you'll never be able to take
all of me.

authors note.

thank you for reading yet another one of my
wild books written from my partying brain
and weeping heart. i hope you enjoyed it,
and i hope you were able to relate to some of
it. writing is a safeplace and it's easier to
write things in condensed little words on
paper rather than voice them to chatty
humans. if you enjoyed this, let me know, i
love to hear feedback.

thank you.

caitlin kelly is a 19-year-old poet, student, and filmmaker. she is the author of *the words of a madman* and *the words i wish i said.* she self-published her first book, *the words of a madman,* at 16 years old. after this, she then self-published her poetry sequel, *the words i wish i said,* a year later, at 17 years old. she was born in amsterdam and has a strong european background and was raised most of her life just outside of los angeles. poetry is her outlet for emotions that she is unable to express out loud. writing is her escape. she plans to continue writing poetry throughout her growth in life. you can keep up with caitlin on her instagram (@c.aitlinkelly) or tik tok (@ca.itlinkelly)